Other titles published as part of the 1992 Ubu Repertory Theater Festival of New French Plays include:

Nowhere by Reine Bartève (Published with *A Man with Women*)

The White Bear by Daniel Besnehard

Family Portrait by Denise Bonal

Jock by Jean-Louis Bourdon

Other individual play titles available from Ubu Repertory Theater Publications are:

Swimming Pools at War by Yves Navarre

Night Just Before The Forest and *Struggle of the Dogs and the Black* by Bernard- Marie Koltès

The Fetishist by Michel Tournier

The Office by Jean-Paul Aron

Far From Hagondange and *Vater Land, the Country of our Fathers* by Jean-Paul Wenzel

Deck Chairs by Madeleine Laik

The Passport and *The Door* by Pierre Bourgeade

The Showman by Andrée Chedid

Madame Knipper's Journey to Eastern Prussia by Jean-Luc Lagarce

Passengers by Daniel Besnehard

Cabale by Enzo Corman

Enough is Enough by Protais Asseng

A Tempest by Aimé Césaire

Monsieur Thôgô-gnigni by Bernard Dadié

The Glorious Destiny of Marshal Nnikon Nniku by Tchicaya u Tam'Si

Parentheses of Blood by Sony Labou Tansi

Intelligence Powder by Kateb Yacine

The Sea Between Us by Denise Chalem

Country Landscapes by Jacques-Pierre Amette

Jean-Marie Besset

THE BEST OF SCHOOLS

translated from the French by

Mark O'Donnell

In Paris, hearts are not given, they are
lent. They are simply experimenting.

Marivaux

She sensed, without being able to
explain it, that he was a victim of that
kind of unreasonable sensibility that
makes men unhappy and deserving to
be loved.

Stendhal

Printed in the United States of America

ISBN: 0-913745-3-40

For Hal J. Witt

The Best of Schools had its world premiere at Ubu Repertory Theater, 15 West 28th Street, New York, NY 10001 on March 3rd, 1992.

Director:	**Evan Yionoulis**
Set Designer:	**Karen Ten Eyck**
Lighting Designer:	**Greg MacPherson**
Costume Designer:	**Francisco Frilles**

Cast, in order of appearance:

Fiona Gallagher	AGNES
Jonathan Friedman	PAUL
Danny Zorn	BERNARD
Mira Sorvino	EMELINE
Gil Bellows	LOUIS-ARNAULT
Justin Walker	MECIR

Produced by **Ubu Repertory Theater**
Françoise Kourilsky, *Artistic Director*

CHARACTERS
(all are young, 18 or 19 years old)

AGNES VOLLAND

PAUL THABOR

BERNARD CHOUQUET

EMELINE DE JOUR

LOUIS-ARNAULT REAL

MECIR

(The kitchen of a student apartment, or at least, the idea of one: its elements are there—linoleum, formica tabletop, unmatched chairs, stools, stainless steel sink and cheap kitchenware—but the room itself is not realistic. The space is vast, and the objects in the room seem lost.

It's late Friday night, almost Saturday morning. AGNES enters and turns on the lights—bright fluorescent white light. She wears stylish pajamas. She opens several cupboards, looking for a pot, finds a dirty one in the sink, washes it, fills it with water, and puts that on to boil. Pause. PAUL enters, as if just awakened. He wears a t-shirt and boxer shorts.)

PAUL: Aren't you sleeping?

AGNES: Did I wake you?

(Pause.)

PAUL: It's ten past three.

AGNES: You want a cup?

PAUL: Of what?

AGNES: Of whatever there is. . . the last mystery tea bag.

PAUL: Tomorrow I'll have to get some groceries. . . I mean. . . Later today. . .

(Pause.)

AGNES: This is taking forever.

4

PAUL: It'll start to heat up all at once. Those things are no good, those electric burners... And then they take hours to cool down... I burned myself the other day.

AGNES: They're all coming back on Sunday?

PAUL: Yes, late Sunday. Or Monday morning.

AGNES: Do you often find yourself alone here all weekend?

PAUL: No, it just happened this way... But I'm not alone as long as you're here!

(Pause.)

AGNES: All three of them went together?

PAUL: Oh no. Chouquet's at his parents'. Vieux's at some kind of convention in Lille. Real's at the regatta in Normandy.

AGNES: With Emeline?

PAUL: I guess.

AGNES: Did they all decide to do this?

PAUL: Do what?

AGNES: Go away all at the same time.

PAUL: They didn't go away all at the same time. They each had their own plans.

AGNES: They decided to have their own plans all at the same time?

PAUL: Look. It's accidental.

AGNES: You just called me this morning. . . All right, yesterday morning, now. . . I could have had weekend plans myself. . . And what if you hadn't been able to reach me?

PAUL: The switchboard did take the message.

AGNES: But on a Friday morning? I might not have checked in. . . I might have left already. . .

PAUL: Left?

AGNES: On some gala weekend, say.

PAUL: But you would have told me, wouldn't you?

AGNES: That's not the point.

PAUL: But you hadn't left. You got the message. You called back. You're here.

(Pause.)

AGNES: I still think all these sudden departures have the air of a conspiracy. . .

PAUL: No, no. Vieux's convention was scheduled a long time ago. Chouquet goes home once a month. It's only Louis-Arnault who decided to go at the last minute.

AGNES: Was it Emeline who lured him away?

PAUL: Lured? They decided to go together, that's all.

AGNES: So you could have the apartment to yourself. . .

PAUL: You have an overactive imagination.

AGNES: To give us free rein. How discreet!

PAUL: If they stayed or left, what's the difference? And what do you mean—"free rein"?

AGNES: I call it as I see it.

PAUL: As you see it? You're looking too hard. Honestly—when they heard about the regatta, they jumped at the chance to go. You know Louis-Arnault. . .

AGNES: I know he wouldn't accept a last minute invitation to this kind of event. And Emeline certainly wouldn't.

PAUL: They weren't sure the races would even take place. It depended on the weather. It's October. The weather's uncertain.

AGNES: Uncertain? I'll say. The Uncertain Conspiracy.

PAUL: Did you have a nightmare or something?

AGNES: No. You have to sleep first to have a nightmare.

(Pause.)

PAUL: Anyway, conspiracy, what are you talking about?

AGNES: Well, plot is more like it.

PAUL: Plot? What plot?

AGNES: Didn't he suggest you call me? Didn't he say something like, "Hey, if you call Agnes, you can spend the weekend together!"... You're not saying anything.

PAUL: Well... even if it was his idea... I could have... I would have gotten the same idea, on my own... You make it sound like...

AGNES: But to make anything happen, it takes Mister Louis-Arnault Real. It takes his approval!

PAUL: That's enough.

AGNES: Maybe not.

PAUL: Look, insomnia makes people irritable... Things get distorted... Tomorrow morning, you'll wake up and see...

AGNES: Oh no. Sleepless nights make you see things clearly. It's daylight that distorts things, all that gray light, and you have to just brace yourself and keep going. At night, everything becomes intense again, you see things for what they are...

PAUL: For you, maybe... But I'm not ready to...

AGNES: You're not?

PAUL: Listen, you're just exhausted, that mattress is too soft. Do you want to try sleeping on the floor?

AGNES: Trade places?

PAUL: If you want to.

AGNES: And you'd sleep in the bed?

PAUL: If you think we'd sleep better. . .

AGNES: Look, there's something we're not dealing with here. . .

PAUL: What?

(Pause.)

AGNES: Is that all you're suggesting, that we trade places?

PAUL: Agnes, if you have any feelings for me. . .

AGNES: Feelings? For you?. . . What do you think I'm doing here? Why do you think, after one little message from you, I cancel all my plans? Yes, my plans. No actual plans, but still, I could have done other things. Don't you even see me anymore? There's nothing and no one besides Real!

PAUL: Look, you're exaggerating. We already talked about this, the other day.

(AGNES seems unimpressed with his sudden violence.)

AGNES: And what did we conclude?

PAUL: *You* concluded that I talk a lot about Real.

AGNES: Louis-Arnault. The other day, we called him Louis-Arnault.

PAUL: All right, that I talk about him a lot. His name did keep coming up.

AGNES: And you claimed that was natural, that maybe you hadn't known him long but you got along so well. . .

PAUL: Yes. . .

AGNES: And since you were out a quarter of the rent, after Vieux's brother bailed out, why shouldn't you suggest to him. . .

PAUL: Well, why not?

AGNES: So, one month after school begins and two weeks after you meet him, he moves in here. In the big room.

PAUL: That's no big advantage. It's also the living room, that's where everyone ends up, to get out of the kitchen. It's less intimate.

AGNES: Then what are we doing in the kitchen?

PAUL: Oh, but. . . that's different. . . He's not here.

AGNES: All the more reason.

PAUL: His things are in there. . .

AGNES: So even when he's not here, he's still here.

PAUL: You're the one talking about him.

AGNES: Me?

PAUL: I admitted his name came up a lot, didn't I? You'll notice that tonight, because of your remark, I didn't mention his name one single time!

AGNES: Yes. You went to such great pains to avoid it, it got. . . .

PAUL: Hey, I talk about him and you complain. I don't talk about him and you complain!

AGNES: Too much or too little, it's the same thing. You just can't be balanced about it. And here I am, and you suggest that I sleep on the floor!

PAUL: Only because you'd sleep better there than in the bed.

AGNES: As if this were all about sleeping!

(Pause. PAUL makes a gesture towards AGNES, to take her hand. She doesn't let him.)

AGNES: I have a bet to make with you.

PAUL: A bet?

AGNES: Let's see which one of us can seduce Louis-Arnault first.

PAUL: What?

AGNES: You heard me.

PAUL: Seduce him?. . .

AGNES: In the classical sense.

PAUL: I am not hearing what I'm hearing!

AGNES: Yes you are.

PAUL: What do you take me for?

AGNES: We've got an obsession here that has to be resolved. I don't see any other solution.

PAUL: You're the one talking about obsession.

AGNES: Oh, you don't even see it. With me, you're gentle and kind and all. . . But when he appears, you're simply. . . transfigured!

PAUL: That's enough! It's not funny.

AGNES: Fine. If you don't want to face it, or admit any of it, I have to conclude that you're more naive than I thought! Well, let's leave it at that. Let's just let things happen. But what was said was heard.

PAUL: I didn't hear a thing.

AGNES: At least let's admit, whether you play this game or not, or if you play it in spite of yourself, without my knowing you are, or without your knowing, even, let's admit that I would be the first to have Louis-Arnault.

PAUL: To have him. . .

AGNES: Right. That I'll show up and say, "I had him."

PAUL: If it's him you want, take him! Why did you come here? I thought we were friends. What's the point in trying to make me jealous? I don't want to get involved in this. . . this. . . You know how I feel. All these years, my feelings haven't changed.

AGNES: That's what I'm complaining about.

PAUL: You're making fun of me.

AGNES: If I win the bet, I'll renounce my prize immediately. And you'll have to as well. This Louis-Arnault, and any other Louis-Arnaults, any Louis-Arnaults yet to come. We'll get an apartment together in Paris, halfway between your school and mine. And we'll never talk about it again.

PAUL: You'd sleep with him, and then want to live with me!

AGNES: On the other hand, if it happens, even without your trying, that you accidentally have Louis-Arnault first, then I promise to disappear from your life, never again to behold the sad spectacle of your indifference to me!

(Pause.)

PAUL: You can't be serious. Tell me you don't mean one word of what you're saying. . .

AGNES: Obviously, Emeline is an additional obstacle. .

PAUL: Come on, stop it, please!

(Pause. They are face to face, motionless. Sound of keys in the front door. BERNARD CHOUQUET *enters, wearing a Burberry raincoat over a black tuxedo. Although he's the same age as the others, he has the voice and manners of a little old man.)*

CHOUQUET: Oh, good evening!... Did I wake you?

PAUL: No... No, you can see, we were here... You know... Agnes....

CHOUQUET: Yes, yes, we've met... Normale Supérieure, wasn't it?

*(*AGNES *smiles.)*

PAUL *(to* AGNES*)*: You remember Chouquet?

AGNES: Sure. Hello, Bernard.

PAUL: I thought you were at your parents'.

CHOUQUET: Yes, I was supposed to spend the weekend in the provinces... And then a friend of my father's invited me to a dinner party... He's a manager at Macipeau Duval.

PAUL: The cheese?

CHOUQUET: Yes, well, dairy products. Second largest in France. And they have investments in phosphates, too.

PAUL: Ah! Phosphates, no less!

14

CHOUQUET: See, he doesn't take the business world seriously.

AGNES: He doesn't take any grown-up things seriously.

PAUL: But I do. Especially phosphates.

CHOUQUET: I won't disturb you. . . I'm just going to have some mint syrup and water. . . Would you like some?

(He mixes some mint syrup with tap water.)

AGNES: No thanks!

PAUL: How was it, this dairy product dinner?

CHOUQUET: Their fiftieth anniversary. They rented the Lido.

PAUL: The Lido? You were just at the Lido?

CHOUQUET: It's not like what they say!

PAUL: The Lido!

CHOUQUET: It's quite spectacular!

PAUL: They had the Lido all to themselves?

CHOUQUET: Of course, what do you think?

PAUL: Macipeau-Duval monopolizing the Lido! What happened to the Japanese?

CHOUQUET: The Japanese don't own the Lido. Besides, there's the Moulin Rouge, the Folies Bergères... Paris is still Paris!

PAUL: Yes, but still, the Lido is the Lido. I bet now they'll boycott Macipeau-Duval cheese in Japan! A total embargo!

CHOUQUET: Everyone on earth can't party at trendy hot spots. That's the point.

PAUL: "Trendy!" It's been at least three and a half years since anyone used the word "trendy"!

CHOUQUET: It was a gorgeous party. And a great show!

PAUL: And isn't it nice to see someone who's just back from the Champs Elysées. No one goes there anymore.

AGNES: Well, excuse me, but I'm going to say good night and...

CHOUQUET: Oh, don't pay any attention to him. With Thabor, you get used to it.

AGNES: You shouldn't let him get away with it.

PAUL: Two against one! I can't win.

AGNES: I'm beat, I'm going to...

CHOUQUET: I understand! Normale Supérieure isn't like here. You really have to work.

AGNES: It's kind of the same everywhere, isn't it?

CHOUQUET: Normale Supérieure is one of *the* best schools!

AGNES: Well, so is this. . .

CHOUQUET: It's not as prestigious, it's not as well-known. . .

AGNES: With the general public, maybe. . . It does have a long history. . .

CHOUQUET: If I didn't like business so much, I'd have gone to Normale Supérieure too. As a beautiful gesture!

PAUL: Notice how he just assumes he would have been admitted!

CHOUQUET: I did consider it.

PAUL: Oh, let's be sincere for a second. What you're saying is, those who do math can do anything, and those who study literature can't do anything else!. . . The Credo of the French bourgeoisie!

AGNES: This is not very entertaining. . .

CHOUQUET: Face facts—the job openings for literature majors are mostly. . .

PAUL: Closed.

CHOUQUET: It's just like anything else. You get out of it what you put into it.

PAUL: What a phrasemaker! Agnes, you must write down what our friend here. . .

AGNES: Good night!. . .

(She exits.)

CHOUQUET: Good night!. . . We're used to him, right?. . .
(to PAUL*)* You made her leave, with your attitude.

PAUL: You couldn't have talked to her, anyway. You're
normal. She's superior.

CHOUQUET: Ha ha. Very funny.

PAUL: And you're patient. Very patient.

(Pause.)

CHOUQUET: Believe it or not, I met someone.

PAUL: Someone?

CHOUQUET: A girl from Centrale that I knew in
school. We'd lost touch.

PAUL: At the Lido?

CHOUQUET: Well, yes, at the Lido, it happened to be
there, but it could have been anywhere else. . . I'd
never seen her looking so good.

PAUL: No?

CHOUQUET: At first I didn't even recognize her. In
high school she was Mademoiselle Nerd. Didn't care
how she dressed, greasy hair, kind of chubby.
Basically a beast. Hardly even female. And now. . .

PAUL: Now, she's dreamy?

18

CHOUQUET: I'll say. I couldn't believe it. She lost
weight. Chic haircut. Nice, classy, a whole new
person.

PAUL: And what about her? Did she recognize you?

CHOUQUET: I know what you're getting at. Well, sure. . .
I wore glasses too, back then. Now I've got contact
lenses. I've got a lifestyle now.

PAUL: Well, all of us, it hasn't been so long. . . The
weird hair, the pimples, the glasses, hitting the
books. We knew it all— national nickel production
country by country, wheat output in Kazakhstan,
integrals, probabilities. All the crucial stuff.

CHOUQUET: And now. . .

PAUL: Well, now!. . . What's her name?

CHOUQUET: Eve, She used to be Yvette.

PAUL: She doesn't like being diminished now.

CHOUQUET: Well, we all change. Why not redo our
names, too?

PAUL: Does everyone change? I don't know about that.

CHOUQUET: You just said. We all had weird hair.

PAUL: Some people already had clean cool hair and
contact lenses, or else good eyes that stayed good.

CHOUQUET: Whatever. Anyway, Eve. I think there's
something there. . .

PAUL: Well, there you go. Something good, despite all that unhappiness.

CHOUQUET: What unhappiness?

PAUL: All those Japanese out in the cold.

CHOUQUET: Oh, right.

PAUL: Going to see her again?

CHOUQUET: I got her number.

PAUL: At her folks'?

CHOUQUET: At her place, she has a studio in Paris.

PAUL: Her own place, her own phone! A bourgeoise!

CHOUQUET: Like us.

PAUL: Speak for yourself.

CHOUQUET: Oh, you aren't?

PAUL: I'm trying to disentangle myself.

CHOUQUET: What are you talking about?

PAUL: I had to come here to realize it, to this school, on this campus. . .

CHOUQUET: Realize what?

PAUL: They invented this system, these fancy schools, to reproduce themselves one notch higher. To push their sons and daughters above the level of shopkeepers. Executives want their sons to be chief executives. Doctors want their sons to head huge German laboratories. Electrical engineers want their sons to rule Silicon Valley. They value those things, they see them as progress. As if it weren't always the same thing, the same crass emptiness.

CHOUQUET: Well, pardon me! But what are you doing here?

PAUL: Hitting my head against the wall. But at least I see the wall is there.

CHOUQUET: Meaning what?

PAUL: I get here, they've got my number—provincial, hardworking, small time. Last week I thought I went out well-dressed, I was told my clothes looked too new! And meanwhile, some people here seem to be another species altogether!

CHOUQUET: Really, I don't see. . .

PAUL: No, of course, you can't see it. . .

CHOUQUET: See what?

PAUL: Their ease, Chouquet. Their nonchalance. Cultured without pushing it, witty but not nasty, light. France As It Thinks It Is. A way of being. All those privileged forebears, polishing them, shaping them, giving them their gleam.

CHOUQUET: That doesn't keep their highnesses from becoming chief executives or managers at Macipeau-Duval.

PAUL: But for them it's without trying, almost without even wanting it. An easiness they get from the beginning, it's a given. For us, just to get where they start from, we have to run, we're already panting.

CHOUQUET: You forget that we're all privileged just by being here. A lot of people would be thrilled to have what we have. Most people even envy us! We passed a major exam that from now on puts a distance between us and them! And that exam is the key. We're enjoying a very high level of education, the highest there is.

PAUL: That's not what you were telling Agnes a moment ago.

CHOUQUET: Oh, Agnes. She's studying literature, that's what she wants. I just wanted to make her feel good.

PAUL: Right.

CHOUQUET: And why not?

(Pause.)

PAUL: Well, the important thing is to believe what you're saying. You're part of the elite, you feel you belong, a pretty girl from Centrale smiled at you!

CHOUQUET: I do feel that way.

PAUL: Of course you've already forgotten she was a fat schoolgirl with gross hair.

CHOUQUET: I was the one who told you about it.

PAUL: Then great, you don't forget a thing. All is well.

CHOUQUET: People change, Thabor. We change. What matters is Now, what we've done with ourselves, where we are.

PAUL: But we'll go on changing, you'll see. What will finally matter is what we turn into. But never mind. All is just swell, isn't it?

CHOUQUET: Oh, it's not so bad here.

PAUL: Goodnight, Chouquet. There's no point in wishing you sweet dreams, since you have nothing but.

(CHOUQUET leaves. PAUL is alone. Pause. Blackout.)

(The scene is the same. Sunday afternoon. AGNES *and* EMELINE *are seated at opposite sides of the kitchen table, reading magazines. What's striking about* EMELINE *is what an archetype she is: blonde, pale complexion, dressed in navy-blue and white, a pearl necklace over a silk scarf. A pause. They read.)*

EMELINE: Shouldn't he be back by now?

AGNES: Yes, but he has to stop by the library, to check on something. . . What about Louis-Arnault?

EMELINE: He went shopping with Chouquet. Louis-Arnault said that since it's Sunday it won't be so crowded.

AGNES: I'd have thought the opposite.

EMELINE: That's what I said. Ever since they've been open on Sundays, it's a madhouse, but. . . it's been quite a while since they left.

(Another pause. They resume reading.)

EMELINE: This magazine has lost 12% of its readership in the past year.

AGNES: Yes, and mine has gained 8% in the same time period.

EMELINE: How do you know that?

AGNES: I already read your magazine.

EMELINE: Ah. *(A pause.)* Did you read the story of this man condemned to death?

24

AGNES: Uh-huh. I read it in yours, and I'm reading the same thing in mine.

EMELINE: The same?

AGNES: Practically. Mine's not so well written, it has the feel of being translated from English.

EMELINE: They gave it six pages in mine.

AGNES: Same here, but fewer photos.

EMELINE: They blow it all out of proportion. . . Once they start with these stories. . .

AGNES: Nonetheless, it's quite a story, isn't it?

EMELINE: Yes. . . I suppose. . .

AGNES: You don't think so?. It's not exactly banal.

EMELINE: It's not the first time. . . All this has happened before.

AGNES: Well, it's the first time I've read a story like it.

EMELINE: Mistrials do happen . . .

AGNES: That's for sure, but like this?. . . Don't you think so? *(A pause.)* Well, don't you?

EMELINE: Oh, I do.

AGNES: You do, what? All this new evidence. . . and they decide not to retry him. . . You think that happens every day?

EMELINE: Not every day, but. . .

AGNES: Then what do you think of it?

EMELINE: What do I think of it? What do you want me to think of it?

AGNES: Well, I don't know. . . I don't know what to believe. . .

EMELINE: You mean, you're not sure?

AGNES: Well, of course not. How could I be?

EMELINE: Why ask what I think, then?

AGNES: Just to get your reaction. . . It's just so incredible, really!. . . Whatever way you look at it. . . Or maybe it's just me. . .

EMELINE: That must be it. I find the case pretty clear.

AGNES: You're kidding. *(Pause.)* Don't you think. . . with men. . . there's always an element of. . .

EMELINE: Of what?

AGNES: I don't know. . . Something like. . . They wouldn't even want to go into. . . it's as if it were a matter of life and death. . .

EMELINE: In this case it is.

AGNES: No, not like that. . . From the start, even. . . They never want to recognize. . . a certain complexity. . .

EMELINE: As far as I'm concerned, he's guilty. *(Pause.)*

AGNES: Which one, the young one?

EMELINE: No no, the other one.

AGNES: Ah. . . Obviously, we don't see things in the same way. . . *(Pause.)* For me, the case they present is incomplete. They've forgotten an element that may play a role in all this. . . Maybe not a huge role, but a role nonetheless. This thirty-eight year old spends the entire day hanging out with this eighteen year old. . .

EMELINE: It's the young one who picked him up, in his car, his stolen car. . .

AGNES: In any case, this man and that boy. . . they go to the drive-in together. . . they spend close to twelve hours together when they don't even know each other. . .

EMELINE: So what?. . . The man is a drifter, the boy's a runaway. . . Two lowlives, killing time. . . guzzling beer in a drive-in. . . Two of a kind. . . bragging. . .

AGNES: Well, the young one. . . No angel, but still, eighteen, young, and not bad-looking. . .

EMELINE: There you go again!

AGNES: What?

EMELINE: Excuse me, but frankly, there you're reading between the lines.

AGNES: And the gun? The implication of the gun? This young man hides it under the front seat, and takes it out to hand it to the older man... This weapon that passes from hand to hand... Any psychoanalyst....

EMELINE: Now you're extrapolating... You're the only one who'd see that in these facts...

AGNES: The only one? Is that so, the only one? On the contrary, I think it's obvious. Obvious. I'm not saying it was crucial to what happened... and yet... who can tell...

EMELINE: You're being completely subjective.

AGNES: Am I? What I'm saying is not even that subtle.

EMELINE: Excuse me?

AGNES: It's plain to see.

EMELINE: I don't know what gets into you when you talk about this, but...

AGNES: About this? Oh... I'm not saying they acted on it... I'm not saying anything happened between them... I'm sure nothing did... All I'm saying is that in all these hours spent together, there's an element... an element that may have escaped the investigators...

EMELINE: But even so... How would that change the investigation?

AGNES: Maybe not the investigation, but...

EMELINE: But what?

AGNES: The meaning.

EMELINE: The meaning! It's always the same with you. I always get the impression you're carrying on about something, and then I realize I don't even know what it is you're talking about!

AGNES: I'm talking about meaning.

EMELINE: Is that so? The meaning of what? There's a death, several deaths, murders. . . pointless ones. . . Maybe there's a mistrial. . . Maybe. The electric chair, maybe. Those are facts. Those are reality. Isn't that enough for you?

AGNES: But it doesn't mean anything.

EMELINE: Maybe not. But it means more than your. . . footnotes! That's what I don't understand with you lit majors! There are things, powerful events, that are right in front of your eyes, and you go searching around for details, little peripheral trivia, that don't really matter!

AGNES: Now calm down. Calm down. We're just having a discussion.

EMELINE: No we aren't. It seems like we're talking about something, but I'm not sure what.

AGNES: There, you admit it.

EMELINE: Admit what?

AGNES: That complexity, that gap, those footnotes that according to you don't really matter!

EMELINE: Listen, let's just leave it at that. I don't follow you. . . I wasn't brought up this way. . . All this arguing. . . . all this picking things apart!

AGNES: We're from different worlds, aren't we?

EMELINE: You're just making things difficult. That's not what life is for.

AGNES: Oh! Well, let me point out that I'm not the one who's getting upset!

EMELINE: Oh, you'd make anyone upset!

(Pause.)

It's true, you have no delicacy. . . You say hurtful things. . . how someone isn't smart, how someone's an idiot. . .

AGNES: I didn't say that.

EMELINE: You implied it.

AGNES: I didn't mean to. I'm sorry.

EMELINE: When I happen to say something that someone doesn't agree with, I change the subject and start on something else, but you, Agnes, if someone contradicts you, instead of dropping it, you dig in, you expand on it, you exhaust it, you become Ultra Agnes! That's what's so irritating.

AGNES: I was wrong. I'm sorry.

EMELINE: No, there's nothing to apologize for.

AGNES: No?

EMELINE: We're different, that's all.

AGNES: That's not what you were just saying. I can see that I have to apologize. I am sorry.

EMELINE: Are you making fun of me?

AGNES: How?

EMELINE: This way of. . . refusing to argue, all of a sudden. . . to back off. . . Excuse me, but it's not like you.

AGNES: No?

EMELINE: No.

AGNES: You say all these things about me. . . I didn't have the impression that we knew each other that well. I, at least, I don't feel like I could say things about you that are so. . . .

EMELINE: What?

AGNES: Well, so definitive!

EMELINE: We don't know each other that well. And if it weren't for the boys, we wouldn't know each other at all. But thanks to them, or because of them, we spend time together. It's not the first time, nor the last, so we might as well. . .

31

AGNES: I'm sorry. I'll do my best so this doesn't happen again.

EMELINE: That's not what I meant.

AGNES: The fact is. . . These moments, that seem harmless to me, at least allow you to get some idea of who I am.

EMELINE: These moments. . . Plus what Louis-Arnault tells me.

AGNES: He talks about me?

EMELINE: Well. . . Your name comes up. . . In passing. . .

AGNES: Oh? *(Pause. Sudden quiet.)* Sure. Why shouldn't it?

(EMELINE waits for a question from AGNES, that doesn't come. AGNES picks up her magazine and resumes reading.)

EMELINE: Good. I'll be off, then. Just tell them I've gone back home.

AGNES: To Maradas Green?

EMELINE: Yes, to my place.

(As she goes to leave, CHOUQUET enters, carrying a big box of groceries, obviously too heavy for him.)

CHOUQUET: Careful. . . Careful. . .

(He puts the carton on the table, clumsily.)

Just in time. . . I just about dropped it. . .

EMELINE: Is Louis-Arnault with you?

CHOUQUET: He helped me load the car, but he said he'd walk back. He wanted some exercise. With all the red lights, I thought he'd beat me back here. He won't be long.

EMELINE: Good, well, tell him I've gone home. If he wants me, he knows where to find me.

CHOUQUET: At Maradas Green?

EMELINE: Where else? What is with all of you, repeating that idiotic name?

CHOUQUET *(surprised)*: Excuse me?

AGNES: That's what the place is called. The lyricism of urban developments. . . .It's not our fault.

EMELINE: All right, I'll see you later.

(She goes. Pause.)

CHOUQUET: What's with her? Did I say something?

AGNES: Not at all. We had a little exchange, that's all.

CHOUQUET *(while unloading groceries)*: I see. It happens. . . It happens. . .

AGNES: "We strangely inconvenience one another. . . " Well, strangely. . .

CHOUQUET: How's that?

33

AGNES: Nothing. I'm quoting.

CHOUQUET *(finishes stocking refrigerator)*: That's nice. Literature is beautiful. . . Me, I never remember quotes. . . It's a frame of mind, I suppose. . . I'm more math-oriented. . . Careful, there's the receipt, there. . . Let's not lose it. . . there's another box. . .

(LOUIS-ARNAULT enters, staggering slightly. He holds his side. A lot of blood is on his shirt and hand. He is very pale.)

AGNES: Louis-Arnault!. . .

CHOUQUET: What happened?

LOUIS-ARNAULT: It's just a scratch. . . It just looks like this. . . because it's bleeding, but it's not. . .

AGNES: Sit down!. . . Wait. . . . *(She exits in a hurry.)*

CHOUQUET: Wow! What happened?

LOUIS-ARNAULT: Oh. . . *(a tired smile)*

CHOUQUET: Really. . . You should've come back with me. . .

(AGNES returns with cotton, disinfectant, bandages. . .)

AGNES: Let's see it. . . Here, better take off your. . .

(LOUIS-ARNAULT hasn't lifted his hand from his shirt.)

LOUIS-ARNAULT *(absently)*: What?

34

AGNES: Your shirt...

CHOUQUET: We'd better call a doctor... *(AGNES helps* LOUIS-ARNAULT *remove his shirt.)* I'll go call a doctor. *(He exits.)*

AGNES: This will tingle, but it shouldn't hurt.

LOUIS-ARNAULT: I am a true and complete idiot. I don't know what came over me. . . .

(Pause. AGNES *disinfects the cut without speaking.)*

I ran into this kid... well... kid... he must have been fifteen, sixteen... in the street... pushing a shopping cart...

AGNES: In the supermarket parking lot?

LOUIS-ARNAULT: No, that's just it, in the street, at the corner by the Science Museum.

AGNES: A full shopping cart?

LOUIS-ARNAULT: No, empty. An empty shopping cart. Stolen, obviously. And I asked him where he'd taken it from.

AGNES: You stopped him?

LOUIS-ARNAULT: Not really, no. I called to him. Not violently. I didn't shout. I think I was even smiling...

AGNES *(without looking at him, absorbed in her task)*: In your best Good Samaritan voice, you asked him where he'd stolen it?

35

LOUIS-ARNAULT: Not really, I said: "Where did you get that?"

AGNES: You blocked his way.

LOUIS-ARNAULT: In going to meet him, I got in front of him.

AGNES: He thought you were blocking his way.

LOUIS-ARNAULT: And he, he took out a knife and jabbed at me.

AGNES: Jabbed at you?

LOUIS-ARNAULT: Well, he stabbed me. I tried to dodge it and he got me in the side. He got away. . . . and it started bleeding. . .

AGNES: And it hasn't stopped bleeding. . . It's deeper than it looks. . .

LOUIS-ARNAULT *(pale)*: It is?. . .

CHOUQUET *(re-entering)*: The phone booth is out of order, naturally!

AGNES: I thought they'd fixed it.

CHOUQUET: It broke again. We'd better go right to the hospital. . .

(LOUIS-ARNAULT is about to faint.)

LOUIS-ARNAULT: Oh. . .

AGNES: Are you all right?. . . Lean forward. . . *(She takes him by the shoulders.)* Lean your head forward. There. . . *(With her hands on his shoulders, she keeps him in the forward position. Pause. PAUL enters.)*

PAUL: What's happening?

AGNES *(to* LOUIS-ARNAULT*)*: Any better?. . .

LOUIS-ARNAULT *(lifting his head)*: Oof. . . . I'll be all right. . .

PAUL: But what's the matter?

AGNES: He was attacked, on his way back from the shopping center.

PAUL: Is it. . . is it serious?

LOUIS-ARNAULT *(weakly)*: Honestly, it's a scratch!

CHOUQUET: They've been trying so hard to make American-style cities here, and they've finally succeeded!

AGNES: It's bleeding a lot. It's more than a scratch.

PAUL: He'd better go to the hospital! What are you waiting for?

AGNES *(looking up, sharply)*: We've just been waiting for you!

LOUIS-ARNAULT: Emeline's not here?

CHOUQUET: He's right. I'll take you right to the hospital.

AGNES: He may need a few stitches. . . .

(AGNES *and* CHOUQUET *help* LOUIS-ARNAULT *to stand.)*

AGNES *(to* PAUL, *who stares at* LOUIS-ARNAULT *as if hypnotized)*: Do you have something to cover him?

PAUL: What?

AGNES: A blanket, to cover him. He's shivering.

PAUL: Oh, right, right!

(PAUL *goes out to get a blanket.* AGNES *and* CHOUQUET *help* LOUIS-ARNAULT *leave.* PAUL *returns with a blanket and sees that they've gone.)*

PAUL: Wait for me!

(He exits after them. Blackout.)

(Monday afternoon. PAUL *and* CHOUQUET *are seated side by side at the kitchen table, which is cluttered with open books and reprints.* CHOUQUET *is absorbed in writing.* PAUL *looks straight ahead. Pause.)*

PAUL: There have always been good little boys, well brought up boys, attentive in school, boys who apply themselves, who can be trusted to go home for lunch. . . And after that, they become good little teenagers, complicated but dressed in the latest styles, with posters hanging in their rooms. . . our rooms. . . which we sometimes lock, and we put a Walkman over our ears, the summit of our anti-social behavior, but we still work hard at school, concentrating on courses, yet with our own little political or poetical preoccupations, just for something extra to talk about. . . but still ready to pass those exams and win those competitions, to take top honors, even. . . And one day it happens! Someone takes out his knife and slash!. . . The little prodigies, these cherished jewels, polished for all those years. . . Hours of piano practice, advanced math, ski lessons, judo classes. . . One jab of a knife here, and another there. . . and the whole world capsizes! Our little world suddenly tilts practically out of sight! And our little brains can't understand it. Always prepared for everything, but not this. Blood on your nice navy blue overcoat! Our little brain suddenly understands just one thing. . . so, all that preparation hasn't been useless, if it understands that it too, could be spattered on the ground, it too, after just one blow, could be nothing but gray jelly. Vaguely disgusting if it gets on your Burberry scarf. And it makes your whole body begin to tremble.

CHOUQUET *(who hasn't raised his head through all this)*: All right. That is quite enough.

(He closes his book and stands.)

PAUL: What?

CHOUQUET: I thought we were going to try to study!

PAUL: Well, go ahead. . . study!

(CHOUQUET takes his materials and leaves in exasperation. Pause. He returns.)

CHOUQUET: This case study has to be turned in by four o'clock. Don't expect to see your name included on it!

(He goes. PAUL is alone, seated, writing. EMELINE enters, a Burberry scarf over her navy blue overcoat.)

EMELINE: What's going on?

PAUL: Nothing. Hi.

EMELINE: I came by to see if there was any news.

PAUL: He's sleeping.

EMELINE: He's sleeping, with all these doors slamming?

PAUL: That's Chouquet. . .

EMELINE: You'd think we were in a play! Did you two have an argument?

PAUL: No. I was just saying that we're all at the mercy of a whimsical Fate, and he stalked out like a madman.

EMELINE: At the mercy of Fate?

PAUL: Yes. After all the sacrifices our families make for us, after all our studies, we're at the mercy of one well-placed stab of a knife!

EMELINE: So he left?

PAUL: Yes.

EMELINE: *You* were talking about the sacrifices our families made for us?

PAUL: I was.

EMELINE: That's not like you.

PAUL: No?

EMELINE: You know, you always seem to think I'm an idiot. . . .

PAUL: No I don't!

EMELINE: When I'm no stupider than any other woman. . . or man, for that matter.

PAUL: What's the matter with you all?

EMELINE: I have to go turn in these reprints. I'll come back in a while. He's not going to sleep all day. . . You and Agnes, honestly, you're made for each other!

(She exits. PAUL sighs. He tries to open a book, closes it, opens it again, and tries to read, his head in his hands. LOUIS-ARNAULT enters, in a white bathrobe with a crest on it, wearing a scarf, in bare feet.)

PAUL: Ah, it's you. Did you get some sleep?

LOUIS-ARNAULT: It was hard to. All these slamming doors, you'd think we were in a play.

PAUL: Chouquet left. Emeline will be by later.

(Pause. LOUIS-ARNAULT gets some aspirin.)

How do you feel?

LOUIS-ARNAULT: I'm slogging along. I've got a fever.

PAUL: Do you need anything?

LOUIS-ARNAULT: What were you all shouting about?

PAUL: It's them. I don't know what's with them.

LOUIS-ARNAULT: And you had no part in all of this?

PAUL: Me? I was talking about you.

LOUIS-ARNAULT: Is that so?

PAUL: I just said that a specimen like you, educated, cultivated as you are, the years it's taken, the effort. . . It's funny that all that could be wiped out with one stab of a knife. . . the whole idea. . . made them upset. . .

LOUIS-ARNAULT: With good reason. Though that idea is not the most original.

PAUL: I don't think the problem was the lack of originality. . .

LOUIS-ARNAULT: It's last week's class.

PAUL: What class?

LOUIS-ARNAULT: The Cost of Opportunity and Risk in Educational Investments.

(Pause.)

PAUL: You're not going to start on this, too, are you?. . .

LOUIS-ARNAULT: What are you working on?

PAUL: A case study for Finance, though working on it may be an overstatement.

LOUIS-ARNAULT: I thought you had teamed up with Vieux and Chouquet for Finance class.

PAUL: Vieux has had it with Chouquet and me. Chouquet has had enough of me, and he doesn't understand much of it anyway.

LOUIS-ARNAULT: Is it that complicated?

PAUL: I don't even understand the first four cases they reviewed in class! Just trying to re-read them. . .

LOUIS-ARNAULT *(sitting)*: Okay, what's the problem?

PAUL: Everything.

LOUIS-ARNAULT: What don't you understand?

PAUL: The title, for starters.

LOUIS-ARNAULT: What? "From Takeover to Leveraged Buy Out"?

PAUL: I must have missed that class.

LOUIS-ARNAULT: The last one, on LBOs?

PAUL: Yes, and the one before, on Takeovers.

LOUIS-ARNAULT: Well, you must have gone to at least one of these classes. . . Yes?

PAUL: In finance? No.

LOUIS-ARNAULT: I see.

PAUL: Yes, you got me, let's forget it. Once I've read the books, maybe, and Chouquet's notes. . . But even then, I don't know if. . .

LOUIS-ARNAULT: LBOs were conceived to counter hostile takeovers. It's a leverage mechanism; the managers of some company anticipate a hostile takeover by allying themselves with financial partners. They buy their own shares, hoping that the rise in the value of the shares is not only going to make up for their investment, but is also going to generate a profit.

PAUL: They buy shares? Where's the money come from?

LOUIS-ARNAULT: Oh, a minimum of actual cash, and the rest is short-term borrowed money from the junk bond market.

PAUL: Right.

LOUIS-ARNAULT: You know what junk bonds are, I assume.

PAUL: Oh, junk bonds, sure, yes, I know them.

LOUIS-ARNAULT: The most spectacular case, of course, was RJR Nabisco.

PAUL: *What* Nabisco?

LOUIS-ARNAULT: You haven't followed the RJR Nabisco buyout?

PAUL: No.

LOUIS-ARNAULT: In 1985, R. J. Reynolds, the tobacco giant, merged with Nabisco, the food giant. . . See, they're the ones who make Ritz crackers, for instance!

PAUL: Right. Crackers. Crackers I understand.

LOUIS-ARNAULT: At the time it seemed like good strategy for the tobacco industry to diversify into food manufacturing. Then, three years later, in the biggest LBO ever, RJR and Nabisco were split up. And the value of the takeover by Kohlberg, Kravis and Roberts—twenty-five billion dollars. Which broke the old record of General Electric over RCA or International Nickel over Electric Storage.

45

PAUL: These are all strictly financially motivated, right?

LOUIS-ARNAULT: Yes. That's one of the objections they have. Some find that it creates too enormous a debt, that it tends to focus managers' attention on short-term profits, it causes drops in productivity, by blocking research and development funding, which aren't really profitable in the short term, et cetera. . .

PAUL: But why bother?

LOUIS-ARNAULT: Some say that it boosts the economy, by putting it in the hands of the financiers. No more bureaucrats, no more inept managers, no more mediocre profits.

PAUL: But what about the factories, the workers, the executives?

LOUIS-ARNAULT: They're in the hands of the financiers. Goodbye, engineering and salesmanship! These days the world belongs to the financiers and business lawyers.

PAUL: But what about the actual economy? Real products?

LOUIS-ARNAULT: Listen, Paul, you're still stuck in the Industrial Revolution.

PAUL: I don't like this.

LOUIS-ARNAULT: What?

PAUL: I just don't like it. It's impossible. I can't get into it. Thanks for your explanations. You're very knowledgeable, you talk about all this with a lot of enthusiasm, excitement, even, but I'm not interested.

LOUIS-ARNAULT: I thought you had a paper to turn in.

PAUL: I won't turn it in, that's all.

LOUIS-ARNAULT: What about your diploma?

PAUL: Exactly. This can't go on. I don't know what's happening to me. I was good in literature, philosophy, English. And I find myself here, listening to lectures about LBOs! I don't know where things went wrong, where I took the wrong turn, but there must have been a moment. . . a moment I didn't see coming.

(Pause.)

LOUIS-ARNAULT: I thought you wanted me to help you.

PAUL: I do. You know what would help me, what would really help me, would be for you to do this paper, and put my name on it.

LOUIS-ARNAULT: You're kidding.

PAUL: It's not a reasonable request, is it? *(Pause.)* How do you manage it, to be so reasonable, to. . . fit in so well?

LOUIS-ARNAULT: I don't like this, Paul. I don't like it.

PAUL: No, I don't like it either. You got a knife in your side. I've got a knife in my head. And I don't know how to help myself. I don't know how you can go on playing the game. . . How you succeed at it. . . I might have done it myself, at one time. But I can't any more.

LOUIS-ARNAULT: Paul. . .

PAUL: I need you, Louis-Arnault. Please don't look down on me.

LOUIS-ARNAULT *(putting his arm around* PAUL'*s shoulders)*: Come on, buddy. . .

PAUL *(breaking away)*: What are you doing? What's come over you?

(He is now standing.)

LOUIS-ARNAULT: What?

PAUL: You know. Don't give me that male bonding stuff. Especially not that. All I'm asking is that gestures mean something, they shouldn't be misleading. If you want to do one thing, don't do the other. Don't seem to want what I seem to seem to want. Just want it.

(LOUIS-ARNAULT, *who can't quite believe his ears, stares at* PAUL. PAUL, *standing at the other end of the room, stares at* LOUIS-ARNAULT. *Pause. Then* PAUL, *without taking his eyes off* LOUIS- ARNAULT, *circles to the door and exits. Blackout.)*

*(Three-thirty on a Thursday morning. The calmness
of night, and its darkness, except for the ghostly
illumination of a streetlight from outside. Someone is
sitting in the darkness. It's AGNES. She goes to the
window, looks outside, and returns. In doing so, she
knocks over a stool. Pause. LOUIS-ARNAULT enters.
The scene reveals itself in "that obscure clarity that
falls from the stars.")*

LOUIS-ARNAULT: Agnes!

AGNES *(softly)*: You'll wake everybody!

LOUIS-ARNAULT: But. . . How did you get in?

AGNES: You tend to leave the door open. That's not
too smart.

(Pause.)

LOUIS-ARNAULT: Does Paul know you're?..

AGNES: No. Anyway, I didn't come to see Paul.
(Pause.) I was at Normale. I studied 'til very late.
This everlasting essay on alienation in American
fiction!.. I stopped at two, and went out to get some
air. . . just to walk in the night. A taxi went by. I
hailed it, it stopped. I took it here.

LOUIS-ARNAULT: You took a taxi here from Normale?

AGNES: Uh-huh. It cost two-hundred seventy-five
francs. Night rate.

LOUIS-ARNAULT: Have you been here long?

AGNES: About half an hour.

LOUIS-ARNAULT: Half an hour, just sitting in the dark?... You should have woke me up... You really should have...

AGNES: I didn't have the nerve. I thought maybe you had a fever, maybe you needed your sleep...

LOUIS-ARNAULT: How long would you have sat there if I didn't hear you?

AGNES: I would have made my presence felt eventually... or else just waited 'til six and taken the first train back to Paris... But that's not what happened, is it?...

LOUIS-ARNAULT: I'm not sleeping very well lately.

AGNES: The stool... was an accident... I didn't mean to..

LOUIS-ARNAULT: Huh?

AGNES: Or maybe I did... Time will tell.

LOUIS-ARNAULT: You might have woken Paul.

AGNES: I don't think so.

LOUIS-ARNAULT: What if you had woken him?

AGNES: There are some things you want so much, at certain moments, that somehow those things happen, and not others... And besides, I didn't intentionally knock the stool over...

LOUIS-ARNAULT: But I thought you just said...

AGNES: I'm saying that the stool wouldn't wake Paul. I'm sure of that. Besides, here *you* are.

LOUIS-ARNAULT: Well, Paul or Chouquet or. . .

AGNES: It's you who woke up. I knew it would be.

LOUIS-ARNAULT: A stool gets knocked over. It's a physical phenomenon. It produces a certain amount of noise—which could just as well have woken the others. All it means is that they aren't such light sleepers as me.

AGNES: Yes, but the *reason* for knocking over the stool. . . All of a sudden I knew that if it were to wake up anyone, it would be you. That it would be you who came.

LOUIS-ARNAULT: You knew it?

AGNES: And maybe you knew, too. . . Did you know I would come, in the middle of the night, that I'd come all this way to see you? That I'd get the urge to go outside, and a taxi would pass by, and I'd have the urge to flag him down, and he'd agree to bring me all the way here. . . See, we've already got a few little miracles here. . . That he'd rush me here, and I'm not exaggerating when I say "rush," this man drove like the wind, he even ran a few red lights, to the point that it became a little. . . eerie. . . if all this happened, then maybe you were calling me too. . .

LOUIS-ARNAULT: I was sleeping.

AGNES: In your dream?

LOUIS-ARNAULT: I don't remember my dreams.

AGNES: But you remember holding my hand all that time, in the hospital. . .

(Pause.)

LOUIS-ARNAULT: I got back together with Emeline. She's here. She's sleeping here, tonight. She's in Vieux's room. He's gone for the week. She's sleeping in his room.

AGNES: But she is sleeping.

LOUIS-ARNAULT: How's that?

AGNES: She's asleep.

LOUIS-ARNAULT: She could wake up, it could happen to her too.

AGNES: Just like she could have come to the hospital with you. But she wasn't at the hospital, was she?

LOUIS-ARNAULT: No.

AGNES: And who was at the hospital?

LOUIS-ARNAULT: You.

AGNES: And Paul, who's also sleeping.

LOUIS-ARNAULT: Paul. Who's asleep.

(In the course of this exchange, they draw nearer each other, each of their gestures contradicting their words. A tender, devilish moment passes between them. EMELINE enters, and turns on the bright

fluorescent light. Dazed by the light, they separate hastily. A pause.)

LOUIS-ARNAULT: You shouldn't have just walked in like that.

EMELINE: So it's not that I was overhearing all this that bothers you, it's that I interrupted it.

LOUIS-ARNAULT: Emeline. . .

EMELINE: It's late, Louis-Arnault. You have a fever.

LOUIS-ARNAULT: Don't use that tone of voice.

EMELINE: You should be in bed.

LOUIS-ARNAULT: Leave us alone.

EMELINE: I wasn't there when you got stabbed, is that it? Because of a few minutes of impatience, patience she made me lose, I've lost you. . . Is that it?

LOUIS-ARNAULT: "Lost!" Please, come on. . .

EMELINE: Well, is it? *She* was there for the return of the warrior! Is it as simple as that?

LOUIS-ARNAULT: It's as simple as that.

EMELINE: She's brought you down to her level pretty fast, I see.

LOUIS-ARNAULT: Emeline, if it had been twenty-five years of marriage, okay, maybe, but not after we've only been going out together for three weeks. . .

EMELINE: I thought we had a sort of intimacy.

LOUIS-ARNAULT: Which doesn't give you the right to make a scene.

EMELINE: The way I feel, I can't help the way it comes out. So it "makes a scene," as you put it!

LOUIS-ARNAULT: All right then, maybe it's what you're feeling that's. . .

EMELINE: It just seemed to me that. . . between us. . . that together, we have. . .

LOUIS-ARNAULT: I know what there is between us. No more, no less.

EMELINE: Oh, of course. This is so easy for you, isn't it?

LOUIS-ARNAULT: Why did you come in here, Emeline? Why do you make us say things like this to each other?

EMELINE: "We've only been going out together for three weeks". . . Is that all there is to it?

(Pause.)

AGNES: Sex attracts people, but it doesn't bind them.

EMELINE: I beg your pardon.

AGNES: Sex is a science unto itself. Like Greek or mathematics.

EMELINE: I'm not talking to you.

AGNES: Men have always known it. Women are just starting to understand it.

EMELINE: So women are acting like men, is that something to celebrate?

AGNES: It is to know you can satisfy your body without any obligations.

EMELINE: To become a slave of sex.

AGNES: To render unto Sex only what it's entitled to.

EMELINE *(to* LOUIS-ARNAULT): I can't believe this!.. Don't tell me you agree with her!

AGNES: When we were at the hospital, he. . . let's say he wanted me. And I wanted him.

EMELINE *(to him)*: And me? What about my wanting you? You didn't always reject me like this! See? I can talk like you all, I can descend to your level too! I can talk like her. I'm talking like her!

AGNES: But I'm being honest. I'm being neutral.

EMELINE: People are attracted to each other, Louis-Arnault. The attraction does finally bind them. They develop feelings for each other. It's always the same feeling. It always comes out in the same way. Finally, maybe it's a difference of sensibility. Or maybe not. It's a difference of talent. Of style. Maybe she has more talent than I do at presenting her feelings. Or at hiding them, maybe. Or maybe she doesn't have any feelings at all.

AGNES: Poor Emeline, you'd think you were in some boulevard drama!

EMELINE: Oh, you're having a good time! Obviously, you're nothing but a spectator!

AGNES: What?

EMELINE *(to* LOUIS-ARNAULT*)*: Don't you see that she's just an observer, that she's always just watching from a distance?

AGNES: I'm here. I'm completely here, it seems to me.

EMELINE: But why are you doing this? Is it some experiment? You watch, Louis-Arnault, we'll turn up as part of her thesis!

AGNES: It's on American fiction. I don't think I could work you in. And besides, it's an essay, not a thesis.

EMELINE: It's a game! She's playing a game!

AGNES: And what of it? I'm playing *the* game.

EMELINE: But you're just playing. You're just playing around.

AGNES: It's a game, you've always got to play somebody!

EMELINE: Not him, at least! *(to* LOUIS-ARNAULT*)* Not you. Am I just playing, am I? Look at me.

LOUIS-ARNAULT: But it had to happen this way, you had to walk in on us tonight. We had to have this ridiculous "scene!" You had to say the things you said! You still have a lot to learn from men. When to keep quiet, for instance. When to act and when to shut up.

(Pause. AGNES *and* EMELINE *are astonished by* LOUIS-ARNAULT's *sudden outburst.* EMELINE *exits, upset.* LOUIS-ARNAULT *and* AGNES *remain. Pause.)*

AGNES: For someone who doesn't talk much, you manage to make yourself understood.

LOUIS-ARNAULT: Agnes. . .

(He comes closer. She backs off.)

AGNES: Excuse me, but suddenly I realize that we don't look at things the same way. . . Women talk, men keep quiet?.. You're just typically phallocentric, aren't you?..

(Pause. They stare at each other.)

LOUIS-ARNAULT: The moment has passed. . .

AGNES: That was such a lovely personal discourse on Desire and Its Obstacles! What an edifying discovery.

LOUIS-ARNAULT: Look, I was disappointed. . . .

AGNES: So was I, but now. . .

LOUIS-ARNAULT: Come on, please. I have a fever. I'm tired.

AGNES: I was wrong to come here. She was right to barge in. Other things would have gotten in the way, anyhow. I'd better leave.

LOUIS-ARNAULT: Would you like to sleep here?

AGNES: Where? In your room? No, I don't think so. If you don't mind, I'll wait here, 'til six o'clock, for the first train.

LOUIS-ARNAULT: You're sure?

AGNES: Yes.

LOUIS-ARNAULT: In any case, Paul will never know anything about this.

AGNES: He won't?

LOUIS-ARNAULT: No.

AGNES: Then all is well, isn't it?

LOUIS-ARNAULT: Yes. All is well.

(He goes. Left alone, she goes to switch off the light. Darkness. She returns to the window. LOUIS-ARNAULT *reappears.)*

LOUIS-ARNAULT: Here. . .

AGNES: What? *(She turns and sees him.)*

LOUIS-ARNAULT: Here, here's three-hundred francs.

AGNES (*turning her head back to the window*): The Penis Returns.

LOUIS-ARNAULT: Look, I have money. All you have is your salary.

AGNES: Oh, well, that's fair. I shouldn't have to pay. After all, we didn't consummate it.

(*At these words,* LOUIS-ARNAULT *slowly tears the three hundred-franc bills in half, and lets them fall to the floor.*)

LOUIS-ARNAULT: If you change your mind, there's some scotch tape in the drawer.

(*He goes. Pause.* AGNES *can be heard crying. Then she resigns herself to gathering up the torn bills. Blackout.*)

(Thursday morning. MECIR enters. He is seventeen and looks even younger. He resembles a child with the manners of an adult. He wears LOUIS-ARNAULT's robe. He tries to work a Walkman, which he's wearing, and finally succeeds. PAUL enters, and goes to the window.)

PAUL: They've gone out. They're all at class. Such good boys. . .

MECIR: Huh?

PAUL: I don't feel like going to classes at all today.

(MECIR puts the headphones back in his ears. Almost imperceptible twanging music is heard. PAUL stretches and looks outside.)

PAUL: To think it took centuries to shape the landscape of Europe. . . The look of the countryside, the boundaries, the fields, the hills. . . But no, they couldn't keep their hands off it. . . Now it looks just like America. . . All you see is ruined landscapes, leveled hills, destroyed forests. . . Everywhere, nature has suffered. . . Look around here. . . Look at what you see from the train. . . When you think of the Impressionists. . . . just a hundred years ago. . . If they could see it now. . .

(As he finishes, PAUL turns to MECIR, who removes the Walkman headphones.)

MECIR: What?

PAUL: I was saying. . . It feels like we're in America.

MECIR: I never been there, to America.

PAUL: I haven't either. But I've seen photos and movies.

MECIR: You never been to America?

PAUL: No. *(Pause.)* I plan to go.

MECIR: Me too. I'm going, someday.

PAUL: Oh yeah?

MECIR *(indicating the Walkman)*: Can I have this?

PAUL: I gave you the watch.

MECIR: But you got it for free, you said.

PAUL: I said that, but. . . Anyway, the Walkman isn't mine.

MECIR *(indicating the robe)*: Well, this isn't yours. You said I could wear it.

PAUL: It's the same with the Walkman. I'm letting you use it. But I can't give it to you.

MECIR: Swatches, they're easy to rip off. . . A Walkman, that's harder..

PAUL: You want some coffee? It's instant.

MECIR: No.

PAUL: There's some biscuits.

MECIR: You're too much.

PAUL: You don't want any breakfast?

MECIR *(laughing)*: Stop!

PAUL: Do you want to wash up?

MECIR: You need it more than me!

PAUL: A shower, maybe?

MECIR: A shower?

PAUL: Or a bath, if you want.

MECIR: A bath, great. At my mother's, there's only a shower. She used to hang things to dry in it, duh!

PAUL: She used to?

MECIR: Yeah.

PAUL: There's a clean towel in there.

MECIR *(indicating the robe)*: Then what's this for?

PAUL: Well, if you want. But use a towel, too.

MECIR *(still about the robe)*: Mustn't get it wet, huh?

PAUL: I'd rather it stayed dry.

MECIR: And the cassette, can I have that?

PAUL: It's not mine either. *(Pause.)* Take it. I'll buy another. Do you have a player?

MECIR: I'll manage.

PAUL: So are you going?

MECIR: I'll split if you want me to.

PAUL: No, I meant to say, to the bathroom.

MECIR *(still toying with the Walkman)*: Right.

PAUL: Your mother is. . . You've lost your mother?

MECIR: She died a week ago.

   (Pause.)

PAUL: Ah. . . I'm very sorry.

MECIR: She had a heart infraction.

PAUL: It was sudden, then?. . .

MECIR: She was a cleaning lady at your school.

PAUL: You mean she was there when?. . .

MECIR: No. That's what she did.

PAUL: So she was part of the maintenance staff?

MECIR: She got up early in the morning to wash the
   floors, the toilets, vacuum the carpeting, clean the
   tables and the chairs. She cleaned each one, one at a
   time, she used to tell me. It gave her backaches.

PAUL: There are a lot of other women on the staff. . .

MECIR: A lot of others to get backaches so you can
   always put your ass in a clean chair.

(Pause.)

PAUL: At least you've had your revenge.

(Pause.)

MECIR: So you like that, huh?

(Pause.)

PAUL: You'd better get going. . . if you want to wash, I
mean.

MECIR: I'll get going, don't worry! I'll get going!

(A wicked grin from MECIR, *who exits.)*

PAUL: It's a strange feeling, this time of year. I usually go back to my parents' for All Saints Day. It's like Christmas—sacred. It's the most beautiful time of the year down there. It's still nice out, the leaves have their fall colors, in the vineyard especially. Walking there, all those bright reds. . . and the pine trees, with that green that's slightly yellow. Walking and talking with my parents. But this year I'm afraid I'd have nothing to say to them. Or, I'm afraid of what I might say. My parents, such nice people, who understand nothing. Only a father's face, or a mother's, has the power to change all of a sudden and leave you feeling. . . To see them look so benevolent, so radiant with fatherly and motherly love, so harmonious, to feel so good with them, so natural, and then, on a single word, to see those eyes turn hard and cold, as if they'd retract your very life, if they could. . . But you're still there. . . I can see them going away, or coming towards me. They're beautiful. They were young once, my parents. I feel like hugging them and saying, "What if we were dogs? What if we were a family of dogs? My parents the dogs. Me, a young dog. Look at me, look at yourselves. I came out of you. We have the same muzzles. And . . . So I've licked the muzzle of another dog, and I've let him lick me! The very same muzzle that you licked so many times after I came out of you. So what? I did it, and for that you're never again going to pick me up by the scruff of the neck and carry me in your mouth? You're going to snarl instead? We'll all bristle and foam at the mouth? No, we're not dogs. We're not even dogs. Mister and Mrs. Thabor. Their son Paul is. . . . you know. . . . But he graduated from a very good school.

(CHOUQUET *enters.*)

CHOUQUET: Talking to yourself? Who is that?

PAUL: What?

CHOUQUET: Who's the guy in the bathroom?

PAUL: Why aren't you at your Macro class?

CHOUQUET: It's the break. I forgot my reprint. Who's in there?

PAUL: It's. . . it's just a buddy of mine.

CHOUQUET: Oh?

PAUL: Uh-huh.

CHOUQUET: Is that what all that noise was, last night?

PAUL: It got late, he couldn't go back to Paris. I suggested he stay over.

(Pause.)

CHOUQUET: I'm going back to class. Oh, if you leave, don't forget to lock up. The door was left open the other night. There've been a lot of robberies lately.

(LOUIS-ARNAULT enters.)

What are you doing here? .

LOUIS-ARNAULT: They canceled Information Systems One. Computer breakdown.

CHOUQUET: What, some virus?

LOUIS-ARNAULT: Oh, yeah, I guess. . .

CHOUQUET: Good for you. I'm going back to class. I was telling Thabor not to forget to lock up when nobody's in the apartment.

LOUIS-ARNAULT: Right.

CHOUQUET: See you later.

(He goes. PAUL *and* LOUIS-ARNAULT *are alone.)*

LOUIS-ARNAULT: First round trip of the day. I don't think I can bear those geometric lawns anymore.

PAUL: Lawns?

LOUIS-ARNAULT: Geometric. The way they cut the lawns in geometric shapes.

PAUL: Where? Here, on campus?

LOUIS-ARNAULT: Yes, on campus. The campus lawns. Crossing those idiotic lawns a million times a day. . .

PAUL: Well, what do you want? Flower gardens?

LOUIS-ARNAULT: That would be better than these dull angles and patterns. It's so green, so perfect, it's boring.

PAUL: It's the geometry that frustrates you?

LOUIS-ARNAULT: Give me some bushes, some underbrush, some forest! Like it used to be.

PAUL: Used to be?

LOUIS-ARNAULT: Yeah. The olden days.

PAUL: It's funny you say that.

LOUIS-ARNAULT: They used to hunt around here. Horsemen, taverns, some ruined castle where you'd find the damsel of your dreams.

(Pause.)

PAUL: Why are you talking about this right now?

LOUIS-ARNAULT: Because I've had to cross these lousy green expanses twice already today. Once in pouring rain.

(Pause.)

PAUL: Louis-Arnault. . .

LOUIS-ARNAULT: What?

PAUL: Nothing.

(Pause.)

LOUIS-ARNAULT: I got this in my mail slot. It's a message from Agnes.

PAUL: She called you?

LOUIS-ARNAULT: Uh-huh. Did she call you?

PAUL: No.

LOUIS-ARNAULT: She didn't call you? Maybe they lost the message. When did you check your box last?

PAUL: Not since last night.

LOUIS-ARNAULT: This message is from yesterday. You'll probably get one today.

PAUL: Well, maybe.

LOUIS-ARNAULT: It's for the party at Normale on Saturday.

PAUL: Oh right. . .

LOUIS-ARNAULT: She probably already told you about it.

PAUL: Not at all. It's news to me.

LOUIS-ARNAULT: I'm sure you're invited.

PAUL: Did she say that?

LOUIS-ARNAULT: Well, I just assumed you'd be going.

PAUL: Uh uh.

LOUIS-ARNAULT: You're not going?

PAUL: I don't know. Nobody asked me. Probably not.

LOUIS-ARNAULT: Now don't do this to me.

PAUL: Do this to you? What? If I'm not invited. . .

LOUIS-ARNAULT: Look, we'll go together. She must have thought, for one reason or another, she could get in touch with me more easily. She knows you don't go to classes much, you go for days without going. . . Maybe the switchboard operators told her you'd gone home for the day.

PAUL: The switchboard operators? Why would they?

LOUIS-ARNAULT: Well, usually you spend a lot of time over there. . .

PAUL: I like the switchboard operators. They're the only people in this whole school who are at all natural and friendly.

LOUIS-ARNAULT: Sure, they're very nice, but. . .

PAUL: But they wouldn't report my movements to Agnes!

LOUIS-ARNAULT You think they wouldn't?

PAUL: Don't talk about them that way.

LOUIS-ARNAULT: You said it yourself, they blab everything.

PAUL: I said they were friendly. At least they appear to be alive.

LOUIS-ARNAULT: Those sweet little ladies know everything.

PAUL: For their personal enjoyment. They wouldn't dream of exploiting it.

LOUIS-ARNAULT: If you say so. . .

PAUL: And furthermore, if they had a message for me from Agnes, they would have seen you this morning, or Chouquet, and they know we all live together, they would have given one of you the message.

LOUIS-ARNAULT: The message is probably sitting in your mail slot at this very moment!

PAUL: Suppose it is. It wasn't there last night. I went to the library at nine o'clock. I checked in when I left. But Agnes did leave *you* a message. That much we know.

LOUIS-ARNAULT: Come to the party, or I won't go either.

PAUL: What for?

LOUIS-ARNAULT: I mean it. What would it look like?.. I don't want to seem like. . . You know, you and Agnes. . .

PAUL: Oh, Agnes and me. . . .

LOUIS-ARNAULT: What?

PAUL: Nothing.

LOUIS-ARNAULT: You *are* friends. She's your friend.

PAUL: Yours too.

LOUIS-ARNAULT: She. . . We're friends, yes. Not in the same way.

71

PAUL: No?

LOUIS-ARNAULT: Definitely not!

PAUL: What do you know about all this?

LOUIS-ARNAULT: Why are you asking?

PAUL: I don't know.

LOUIS-ARNAULT: You two have known each other since. . .

PAUL: A long time.

LOUIS-ARNAULT: She's your best friend.

PAUL: Oh? A woman can be your best friend, or for that matter she can be your girlfriend, the adjectives are a little ridiculous. Who'd want to be anything other than best?.. Still, it's easy to see which they prefer.

LOUIS-ARNAULT: Whatever, suit yourself. So you'll come on Saturday.

PAUL: Saturday again? Look, I honestly believe that Agnes wants you to go to her party. I also believe she doesn't want me to go.

LOUIS-ARNAULT: Why, what did she tell you?

PAUL: Tell me, about what?

LOUIS-ARNAULT: About me.

PAUL: We haven't even talked since you were in the hospital.

LOUIS-ARNAULT: What about at the hospital?

PAUL: Well, it seemed like, at the hospital, you mostly talked to each other.

LOUIS-ARNAULT: Is that what it is?

PAUL: What what is?

LOUIS-ARNAULT: There's nothing else bugging you?

PAUL: Like what, for example?

LOUIS-ARNAULT: You're off track here, there's nothing going on.

PAUL: No?

LOUIS-ARNAULT: And besides, I've got Emeline!

PAUL: Emeline?

(MECIR *enters, dressed in torn black jeans, a belt, a shirt. When he sees him,* LOUIS-ARNAULT *bolts to his feet.)*

LOUIS-ARNAULT: Whoa! *(He backs up.)*

PAUL: What is it?

LOUIS-ARNAULT: That's the guy! The guy with the knife!

(LOUIS-ARNAULT brandishes one of the stools like a weapon. Pause. MECIR takes a knife from his pocket.)

PAUL: No, wait! Stop!

LOUIS-ARNAULT: Once, but not twice!

(A menacing pause. LOUIS-ARNAULT, stool in hand, makes MECIR back off. PAUL doesn't speak, fascinated. LOUIS-ARNAULT knocks the knife from MECIR's hand. They're face to face on opposite sides of the table. PAUL picks up the knife and blocks LOUIS-ARNAULT's way. MECIR takes the opportunity to escape.)

PAUL: Leave him alone!

LOUIS-ARNAULT: You are nuts! You're completely insane!

(PAUL and LOUIS-ARNAULT are face to face. A pause. Blackout.)

(Sunday. PAUL is seated, daydreaming. A box is on the table. In one corner, several suitcases. EMELINE enters. A pause.)

EMELINE: Louis-Arnault told me to tell you he's moving to another apartment. So, you can look for another roommate.

PAUL: So this is it?

EMELINE: Yes, you'll have to look for a replacement.

PAUL: No, I meant. . . He told you to tell me. It's come to that?

EMELINE: Look, Paul, it's none of my business, but. . . I don't see what's so surprising.

PAUL: That he hasn't spoken to me for three days. That he should leave like that. . .

EMELINE: How could he stay, after. . . Everybody on campus is talking about nothing but this.

PAUL: If they find it so fascinating, maybe it's because they don't have anything going themselves. . .

EMELINE: Of course, it's always other people's fault, never yours.

PAUL: Never mind them. But that he. . .

EMELINE: He's not so different from them.

PAUL: I had thought. . .

EMELINE: Oh, you thought. We all like to think.

75

PAUL: Don't tell me it's what other people think that made him decide to. . . .

EMELINE: Really, Paul, are you so out of touch with. . . Is your grasp of things so weak?

PAUL: And your grasp of things, Emeline, is it that keen?

EMELINE: What do you mean?

PAUL: What do you think?

EMELINE: I don't have a clue.

PAUL: It seems to me that not so long ago, in circumstances not so very different, you weren't quite so sure of yourself.

EMELINE: I don't know what you're talking about.

PAUL: Don't you? Wednesday night. . .

EMELINE: He told you?

PAUL: I heard you.

EMELINE: That has nothing to do with this.

PAUL: No?

EMELINE: What, that Louis-Arnault had a. . . a fling with Agnes? That I suspected him? And caught them at it? There's nothing so unusual in that. . .

PAUL: Ah, so, for you, it was all very conventional.

EMELINE: How do you mean?

PAUL: Right. Basically, a familiar situation. It could have happened to your mother, or your grandmother. . . So, your own life isn't all that specific, your own ideal of Louis-Arnault didn't matter all that much. None of this is personal. It's cultural, isn't it?

EMELINE: I don't see the connection. You came to the defense of this. . . this person who could have killed him! Frankly, there's no comparing. . .

PAUL: Obviously , you have your own way of not looking at things.

EMELINE: Talk about not looking at things. . .

PAUL: It's a question of emphasis, of point of view. What one chooses to say, or notice.

EMELINE: What are you getting at?

PAUL: You have something against me. You're kidding yourself if you think I'm the bad guy. We're in the same situation, Emeline.

EMELINE: Is that so? I at least have friends. I have Louis-Arnault. You, you're alone. Everybody else is against you.

PAUL: Again with everybody else, with other people. Get over it, Emeline.

EMELINE: Other people are important.

PAUL: Other people, they're like the daily news. They're like the paper I get every day and never open.

EMELINE: That doesn't make sense.

PAUL: No. It's not others we need. It's one other. Without that we're alone, and the world still goes on. I'm alone without Louis-Arnault. And there you are, alone with Louis-Arnault. Your friends and your parties and your regattas and the babies you'll have, those won't cure your solitude, Emeline. All those will only reassure those other people you're talking about. You're alone, from now on, with the real Louis-Arnault. The man you dreamed of, you lost him Wednesday night.

EMELINE: You don't even know him. You can't imagine. . . .

PAUL: What can't I imagine? Your reconciliation? How at some point he came to see you and got all grand and misty ? How tender he was? How touching? How he vowed, and promised, and almost but didn't quite cry? I can imagine, Emeline, I can imagine. I know how he can be. . .

EMELINE: You talk about him as if. . .

PAUL: That's right.

(Pause.)

Why did he leave? Why won't he even speak to me anymore?

EMELINE: Because he can afford not to.

PAUL: Can he? Well, he's wrong. I can handle this.

EMELINE: I can't even believe we're telling each other these things.

PAUL: That's because we're talking in a way two people can talk only once in their lives, when they know they'll never see each other again.

EMELINE: We still have another three years at the same school.

PAUL: I'm sure we'll pass each other on the geometric lawns.

EMELINE: It'll be a little embarrassing, won't it?

PAUL: Oh, no. It'll be like we don't know each other.

EMELINE: You think?

PAUL: You'll see. And you'll do it very well.

(Pause. CHOUQUET *enters.)*

CHOUQUET *(to* EMELINE*)*: Well, well, how are you doing?

EMELINE: Hi.

CHOUQUET: The pay phone is still broken. It's enough to drive you crazy.

PAUL: But it was working again on Friday.

CHOUQUET: I'd like to know who broke it!

PAUL: What for?

CHOUQUET: Probably some friend of yours. . . .

PAUL: Okay, enough with that!

CHOUQUET: He's very good at going at humans with a knife. I don't see why he shouldn't smash up telephones too.

EMELINE: Well, I guess I'll be going. . .

(LOUIS-ARNAULT enters.)

LOUIS-ARNAULT: Oh good, you're still here. I wondered what you were doing.

EMELINE: I'm just leaving.

LOUIS-ARNAULT: I was just thinking you couldn't carry everything by yourself.

CHOUQUET: Did you find someplace?

LOUIS-ARNAULT: Not yet. But the agency's optimistic. I'm staying at Emeline's. And anyway, I can always spend a few days at my parents' in Paris while I'm looking.

(He deliberately ignores PAUL, and seems very comfortable.)

EMELINE: Well, you can stay with me as long as you like.

CHOUQUET: I looked for you at the party at Normale last night.

EMELINE: We didn't feel up to it.

LOUIS-ARNAULT: How was it, fun?

CHOUQUET: A lot of fun. Those literature majors know
how to party.

EMELINE: Do they?

CHOUQUET: Agnes Volland took charge of me. She was
dancing like a madwoman! Everybody got into it. I
think she was a little smashed. After that I couldn't
really get away from her. She recited her thesis
to me.

EMELINE: Once she gets started. . .

CHOUQUET: Exactly. Literary types.

PAUL: Alienation in American Fiction.

(Everyone ignores his comment.)

CHOUQUET: She's up to Lobotomies in the Nineteen
Forties!

LOUIS-ARNAULT: A lot of people had them done back
then, so they say. Didn't one of the Kennedy
daughters get one?

EMELINE: That's right. Rosemary. Her father had it
done without telling her mother. He took advantage
of the fact that she was away at some spa to have it
done, but something went wrong. When she got
back, the mother could tell that something had
happened. . .

LOUIS-ARNAULT: You're certainly up on this subject.

EMELINE: It was Agnes who told me about it!

CHOUQUET: And something I didn't know, was that the inventor of the lobotomy. . . I forget his name. . . He got the Nobel Prize!. . . And in the end he was assassinated by one of his patients. . . Some woman he'd done one of the very first lobotomies on, he'd written a big essay on her that won the prize. . . She was the one who killed him.

EMELINE: Agnes loves those kind of stories.

CHOUQUET: You have to admit. . . Well, it's quite a story!

(AGNES *enters, pale, with drawn features.*)

AGNES: I see I wasn't merely lecturing to a vacuum!

CHOUQUET: Agnes! I was just talking about you.

AGNES: Yes, Bernard. That's what it sounded like.

CHOUQUET: Talk about coincidental!. . .

EMELINE: I didn't know you were coming down this weekend.

AGNES: No, neither did I. Anyway, the weekend's over.

CHOUQUET: It's amazing we're still standing, after last night!

AGNES: Is it? I haven't even been to sleep yet.

CHOUQUET: What? After last night?

EMELINE: I'm sure you can handle one more sleepless night.

AGNES: I went to the movies this afternoon in Paris. To make Sunday go by.

EMELINE: What did you see?

AGNES: An American film.

CHOUQUET: I'm with you there! Give me an American movie!

AGNES: A horror movie.

CHOUQUET: Oh? I'm not crazy about horror movies. How about you all?

AGNES: Around Saint-Lazare, there's not much choice.

EMELINE: There are plenty of porno movies in Saint-Lazare.

AGNES: Yes, that and horror.

EMELINE: I'm sure it's the same clientele.

PAUL: What were you doing in that neighborhood?

AGNES: I was walking around in the train station, and I wasn't sure about coming down here. I watched all the morning trains leave. Two every hour. One at twenty-three after, one at fifty-three after.

EMELINE: Thank you, we know the schedule!

AGNES: So I went to the movies. I saw two horror films. In the second one these monsters without eyes start a panic out in some desert. The couple next to me were making out.

EMELINE: Just like I said.

AGNES: When I left around four o'clock, the sunlight was so sad that I just got on a train and came here.

EMELINE: The four twenty-three. And here you are.

(Pause.)

LOUIS-ARNAULT: Well. . .

CHOUQUET: You going?

LOUIS-ARNAULT: Yes. About the rent, we can work that out.

CHOUQUET: Right, right, of course.

(LOUIS-ARNAULT crosses in front of PAUL to get his bags. He picks up his suitcases.)

LOUIS-ARNAULT *(to* EMELINE*)*: Would you get the carton? It's light.

PAUL *(to* LOUIS-ARNAULT, but facing the others): You know, basically, I'm not sure what you're after, this whole future you're heading into, I'm not sure it's so very honorable, or even very manly.

CHOUQUET: What? What is he talking about?

AGNES: I don't think he's talking to you, Bernard.

PAUL: Maybe I have some ancient outmod
honor, I don't know. . .

EMELINE: Code of honor?

CHOUQUET: What is he talking about?

EMELINE: The Crusades, no doubt.

PAUL: That's what it's all about, isn't it? To be a wiz at
finance, and financial law, to look down a little on
marketing, or the other way 'round, it's all a little bit
vulgar, finally, isn't it?

EMELINE: Manly? You're talking about what's manly?

PAUL *(still to* LOUIS-ARNAULT, *who hasn't budged):* I
don't know, but it seems to me, well, when we met,
you talked to me about Chateaubriand and Kipling
and Conrad. I talked to you about Michel Foucault.
We used to talk. You took my breath away. I felt
high with you, I felt. . . And now, the other day,
when I saw your eyes light up when you were going
on about LBOs and Nabisco food products!. . .

EMELINE: But this manly business, Paul, explain that.

PAUL: Mister Future Financier, business lawyer in an
international firm. Suites in the Hotel Nikko,
business dinners with panoramic views in
Montparnasse Tower, seminars in Holiday Inns,
contracts, banquets, call girls in soundproof rooms
with air-conditioning and champagne mini-bars!
What a life, huh? Is that what life should be?

CHOUQUET: What's he saying? What has he got
against the Hotel Nikko?

85

NES: Well, come on! You're not going to let him just say that, are you? You're not going to let him put down your career? *(to* LOUIS-ARNAULT*)* Say something! Say something to him! What is going on here, if someone like you can't even respond to him?

LOUIS-ARNAULT *(cold and calm):* What do you want? Should I punch him out?

AGNES: But you're just sitting there! Don't you know how to answer him? You must see that he's only pointing out the most trivial details of the career you're planning! He's only talking about trappings, externals, and he's forgetting what's really at stake: the negotiating, the psychological warfare, getting those signatures, keeping secrets, the strategy, the battle, the victory, ultimately noble things! Can't you tell him that? Don't you even know it yourself? *(to* PAUL*)* And what are you going to do that's so great? You'll end up working, you'll get a job, won't you? You'll end up an executive, won't you, Paul? You'll be fully executed, won't you?

EMELINE *(to* LOUIS-ARNAULT*):* That's the way they are. They're both the same, the two of them. They have to dissect everything endlessly.

AGNES: You wouldn't mind if he did punch him, would you? The good old-fashioned way.

EMELINE: It seems to me it was Paul who talked about what was "manly." He was the one who used that word.

PAUL: I said that word. I'm not sure you understood it.

EMELINE: Maybe you think that you just have to use a word to change its meaning. . .

AGNES: At last! See, Louis-Arnault, your beloved Emeline has at least articulated an idea here! I'll bet you could, too, if you tried!. . .

(Long, heavy pause. LOUIS-ARNAULT *crosses the stage with his suitcases and goes.* EMELINE *takes the carton and follows. Pause.* CHOUQUET *exits as well.* AGNES *and* PAUL *remain. A pause.)*

AGNES: So?

PAUL: So?

AGNES: So I could have had him.

PAUL: But you didn't have him.

AGNES: No. I hesitated. I was thinking of you.

PAUL: Oh really?

AGNES: Yes, what do you think?

PAUL: What do I think? You hesitated to win your bet, you hesitated to take the train. . . You claim you're more hesitant than maybe you really are. . .

AGNES: I'm just thinking of you.

PAUL: Still, according to your bet, we had to take it all the way. We had to say, "I've had him."

AGNES. I thought you'd pretended not to understand. I thought you'd refused to play.

87

PAUL: But you were all set to. . .

AGNES: I did hesitate. Besides, the stakes were pretty pathetic, as it turned out, weren't they?

PAUL: That's not what you seemed to think just now. . .

AGNES: The poor thing. He was standing there. . . And you were going at him. . . He needed a little help. . .

PAUL: He didn't seem so pathetic to you on Wednesday night . . .

AGNES: Oh. . . *(Pause.)* You heard all that?

PAUL: It was hard not to.

AGNES: Bernard slept through it. The doors were closed.

PAUL: Chouquet puts plugs in his ears. And a mask, like they give you on airplanes. Chouquet barricades his head before going to sleep.

AGNES: You heard everything?

PAUL: Not everything, no.

AGNES: Then you know I did hesitate.

PAUL: It was Emeline's voice that woke me. You didn't stop yourself. She interrupted you.

AGNES: It was only for your sake that I would have gone all the way.

PAUL *(shaking his head)*: Agnes, Agnes. . .

(Pause.)

I had him. I had Louis-Arnault.

AGNES: What's that?

PAUL: You heard me.

AGNES: Chouquet told me that you two had a fight. Besides, he's moving out, isn't he?

PAUL: Did Chouquet tell you why?

AGNES: He just said you had a fight.

PAUL: Well, that's why we fought.

AGNES: When did all this happen?

PAUL: Thursday. He was kind of drunk. He came to me.

AGNES: He was drunk, he came to you, you took advantage of it. You expect me to believe you?

PAUL: Yes.

AGNES: Why would he have been drunk? It's not like him.

PAUL: To give himself an excuse to give in to what he wanted to do.

AGNES: He did nothing of the kind. I don't think he wants anything like that. I'm just about certain he doesn't.

PAUL: You're right to say "just about."

AGNES: So it was him who came to you?

PAUL: Something was missing on his reprint for class. He wanted to read mine. At two in the morning.

AGNES: Sure, like you're always working deep into the night. . .

PAUL: We do work late here. We were going through the chapter. He let his hand touch me. And he didn't move it.

AGNES: That's not true, Paul. You're lying.

PAUL: Am I?

AGNES: Louis-Arnault is nothing like that.

PAUL: But there is a part of the masculine personality. . . which is. . . merely. . . mechanical.

AGNES: Mechanical?

PAUL: It doesn't matter whose the hand is, if it's a caress. If all you want is a response.

AGNES: You aren't shy about giving details.

PAUL: That's because that one detail says more than all the rest. That one detail that lets you know the line is being crossed.

AGNES: I must be a pretty amateurish lover, then, if when I'm with you I can't even get you to respond. . . mechanically.

PAUL: It wasn't always the case.

AGNES: Oh. . . I wanted you to want me too much.

PAUL: I don't think Louis-Arnault is going to want me again. But Thursday. . . One time, anyway. . . Once in his lifetime. . .

AGNES: Once was all that was called for.

PAUL: It's you who made the rules.

AGNES: I don't believe this. I don't believe one word of this whole story.

PAUL: You'll have to take my word for it.

AGNES: Well, that's that, then. You have what you want.

PAUL: It's you who told me what that was, Agnes. It's you who rushed me into this.

(Pause.)

AGNES: Tell me it isn't hopeless.

PAUL: I don't know.

AGNES: We still have our conspiracy, our amazing complicity. You confide things to me that are very seldom spoken. I listen to them and I tell myself that you're not telling me all this in order to hurt me. I try to find them harmless, without malice, honest. Between a man and a woman, nothing could be closer than the bond we share.

PAUL: What about. . . desire?

AGNES: Is that closer? Well, one body may be taken by another. . . for a moment. . . there's great heat. . . It's all a little raw. . .

PAUL: Maybe that just can't be helped.

AGNES: Well, then, it's finished, isn't it, Paul? It's finished.

(PAUL goes to the table. LOUIS-ARNAULT's Walkman has been left behind. He puts the headphones on his ears. He turns on some music. He seats himself exactly as MECIR was. AGNES stares at him, and exits. Blackout)